I0689438

Aspiring to Ritual:

One Hundred Sonnets

Kevin M. Clay

Romar Press

Romar Press

3157 CR 518, Stephenville, Texas 76401
publisher@romarpress.com
www.romarpress.com

Copyright © 2025 by Kevin M. Clay

Cover art: *Person Behind Fog Glass*
Photo by Stefano Pollio on Unsplash

Hardcover: ISBN 979-8-9921836-4-1
eBook: ISBN 979-8-9921836-5-8

All rights reserved.
This publication may not be reproduced in whole or part in any form.

Dedication

For more family . . .

Matthew Jacob Clay

Rae Elizabeth Clay

Theodore Raymond Clay

Alison Love Mendoza

Isaiah Alexander Mendoza

Lauren Pink Clay

Violet Edna Clay

Zack Luna Clay

Gregory Mark Clay

Charlene Inez Clay

Alejandro Simon Clay

. . . And those to come . . .

Acknowledgements

Holman, C. Hugh "Quatorzain." *A Handbook to Literature*. 6th edition. New York: MacMillan Publishing Company, 1992. 389.

ii

Weiskiott, Eric. *English Alliterative Verse*. Cambridge Studies in Medieval Literature. 96. Cambridge: Cambridge University Press, 2016.

Weiskiott, Eric. "Introduction." *Alliterative Verse / Avant-Garde*. Poetry Foundation. December 12, 2022. https://ericweiskott. com/2022/12/13/alliterative-verse-avant-garde/.

Foreword: A Brief Note on the Sonnet

A sonnet is usually thought of as having a brief list of requirements. For my own practice, I have used these. A sonnet typically:

1. Consists of fourteen lines in any meter
2. Features an end-stopped rhyme scheme
3. Shows a pivot or other disruption as it draws to its end
4. Can be divided variously into couplets, triplets, quatrains, sestets, and even octaves
5. Concludes decisively and with rhetorical force

The earliest sonnets I know of are those of Giacomo da Lentini in 13th-century Renaissance Sicily. That said, the sonnet's history is nothing if not argumentative and inventive—as in the present case, where I have opted to work in what may be loosely called the *blank sonnet* or the *quatorzain*—sonnet-like forms identical to the above except in the blank sonnet, without rhyme. The first blank sonnets were written by Henry Howard, Earl of Surrey, in the 16th century, sometime before he managed to lose his head.

There are rubs, of course. Taken together, everything—*everything*—that can be said about the sonnet ultimately concludes with an acknowledgement of extensive variation while struggling to finalize and carve in marble a set of implicitly inviolable cut-and-dried rules and definitions. This occasions, in my view, a powerful *creative tension* that many writers have found productive. Certainly, poets as widespread in period, style, subject, and nationality as Petrarch, William Butler Yeats, and Richard Wilbur have all written sonnets, regularly at variance with prescriptions of whatever source, so that although retaining most often the use of those rhyme schemes and of fourteen lines of Iambic Pentameter, vary in other ways, too. My own opinion is that the mythic and "true" sonnet—true in Plato's sense—doesn't exist. It's like a "pure race." There just isn't one.

Even Petrarch in *Canzonieres* used meters other than the iambic, and lines other than pentameter, and even lyric forms that were decidedly not sonnets, or even sonnet-like. Many have noted that the many "sonnet forms" are variations of Petrarchan or Elizabethan practice—but there is also the *quatorzain* to consider. The quatorzain, we are told, derives from the French *quatorze*, and consists of fourteen lines, like a sonnet. Holman and Harmon define the quatorzain as "A stanza of fourteen lines. The term is usually reserved for fourteen-line poems not conforming to one or the other of the sonnet patterns."

What we are accustomed to style as Elizabethan sonnets, of course, *always* end with a couplet, and sometimes, rather than three quatrains, it can be two sestets and a couplet, or an octave, a quatrain and a couplet. Furthermore, they have very specific rhyme schemes, typically of ABAB CDCD EFEF GG, as is well known. The seminal English sonnets of Henry Howard and others may well be quatorzains, and I'm OK with that—but *these* quatorzains are sonnets by such long and distinguished usage, it is in my view a false claim on its face to say they are not. This whole business is quite the mess, really, not lending itself readily to any promulgation of absolutes.

Thus further, I am happily at variance with the various classical requirements of any and all of the variegated sonnet types, in ways well beyond lack of rhyme. Whether Petrarchan or Shakespearean lack of rhyme or even the Spenserian form that few ever mention at all, who knows? Of course, English is sometimes a challenging language in which to rhyme, especially the old Germanic English—this, too, is well known. Perhaps rhyming did not give a Shakespeare or Dylan Thomas or sonnetless Chaucer much trouble, but I would note, nevertheless, their not infrequently tangled syntax as a sign that it did kick up *some* trouble, at least, for those same distinguished poets. In any case, with all this variation in the storied past, I am at ease with my belief that "pure" sonnets—so-called—simply do not exist, but are conflated, bastardized, revised and adapted endlessly, a true motley in aspic, across four and more centuries.

I still have other reasons why I think this. We speak of such variations without so much as a blink, do we not? And probably mean to. Pointing to such affinities between *St. Erkenwald* and Elizabeth Willis' "Tiptoe Lightning," in his book *Alliterative Verse/Avant-Garde*, Eric Weiskott of Boston College finds odd but informative likenesses between Medieval Anglo-Saxon Alliterative Verse and 20th and 21st century lyric poetry, so resolutely *vers libre*. He asserts further that "the two bodies of poetry belong together because, for 21st-century readers, they both push the envelope of what poetry can be and do."

I say we need more of that.

I think that the complex and repeated and practically endless qualifications we encounter give us ample practical leeway regarding what is and is not a sonnet. A number of my lines run to fourteen syllables—a heptameter—a matter of seven iambic feet; a few are thirteen or fifteen lines long, rather than the customary fourteen. It is true also that rhyming in English is a headache—but as noted, they did not rhyme at all in Old English, using alliteration—or we are seeing from Weiskott and others now, marking stresses with alliteration—and seem not to have been diminished thereby. I also freely break these lines into sections— or not—couplet, tercet, quatrain, sestet or octave, as seemed fit to me. For me, English finds its forms more easily and effectively in so many other places than rhyme, and I daresay others must feel the same.

Geoffrey Chaucer introduced us decisively to rhyme in the 14th century with his use of Italian and French models—Romance languages in which it is much, much easier for rhymes to be made than in Germanic English. In all of this, I desire only the freedom to innovate further. And so: we know a sonnet is usually thought of as having a brief list of requirements. For my own practice, they are much the same as the ones given before—except that I am (if rarely) sometimes below or above the fourteen-line limit. A sonnet here can be in any meter; and of course, as blank sonnets, they do not rhyme.

I am a lover of sonnets—I extravagantly relish the work of Petrarch and of Howard, Wyatt, Shakespeare, and Sydney. I enjoy equally the Modernist sonnets of Yeats, and of Richard Wilbur, and of others. I have attempted my own many times. One day after the turn of the century, I sat down, and these blank sonnets just commenced to gush out. I have tinkered with them for many years now. I find the blank sonnet a flexible, versatile and congenial medium in which to work with seriousness. The form in general brings with it a *gravitas* all its own, especially in its division of issue and/or problem posed, and solution and/or resolution proposed. My personal obsessions, of course, with love and death—the only two subjects, really—and most consequentially, with time, so wrapped up in those other two—crop up everywhere. I have happily lingered over them at great length.

"Farewell my book, and my devotion," Chaucer wrote. Time has run down at last to that point for my own modest efforts. So here is my gift to the world, for all good and ill as may be. It is my hope that these 100 are the best of the lot. I, therefore, with hope, commend them to your attention.

Arlington, Texas
2025

TABLE OF CONTENTS

Aspiring to Ritual:

One Hundred Sonnets

Kevin M. Clay

Aspiring to Ritual

That savage god lives in the gray sea—the
trough nearer the deep, the peak whipped to
white foam, a swell from as far as Cornwall,
over deeps as black as the true night of caves.

Unknown. Unknowable. For us it comes
to antic shadows in garish colors. These
cavort across glowing screens, and nothing
depends on them. Deluded into belief, some

import of affection, that *will* change. Is it
pretense puffed up into art? Proportionate to
that degree within it aspiring to ritual. I might have
chosen that path. Painted and preened like it matters.

In all the cruelty and pain of creation. But
nothing is made, if it is not made to be broken.

2016

Flash Flood

Water sluices over earth, a flash flood over old
stone. Fire thirsts desperately for water.
There are clouds on the far horizon, clean, and

full of all that wicks up from salt seas. I must
remember, what has been born hard is not
always bitter, like the breath of God's passing.

Pass on. I could step outside these walls and
slabs of gross flesh, and float away. West
toward the sun. Do maidens await me there?

Let the waste within be soaked in tides,
the flinty sand and edged obsidian shards
stroked smooth by water. I am so long

the anchorite wheezing dry, futile prayers,
lost in the hermitage of devouring time.

2005

Lustful Prince

The whores were as ever, avaricious and sweet.
They swallowed the salty and essential contradiction.
Just so the Prince from Wittenburg told you,
get thee to a nunnery, and quickly, too, in order to be
safe therein. But also thoroughly and deeply fucked.
Profane or holy, we all know abundant lubricant

remains always the truly needful thing. I went
to the temple, filled with beautiful women. I paid
out money in the soft air of dawn. Fuck them,
and this is a hymn. An act made holy by the
foaming flesh, where frolic lubricious satyrs,
nymphs, and other lustful fauna. I had a girlfriend.

I loved her. A tumult of insanity.
Fucking her was like singing a high mass.

2014

It Stinks of Truth

The blade is poised to carve the profile,
though I do not say whence nor why.
It takes me into the dark. I wish
it would go somewhere else, but that is where
it takes me. A damp cave. Underneath
a table, until the fight is done.
And then it jerks me into light.
The glow and glare of a torch flares like
an inner burn, less whimper than sigh,
the more wretched that it stinks of truth.
The bloody chunk of a tumor coughed
into seeing. Wet, crimson, glowing.
Steam curls off its surface; time runs out,
as time will. Sweet prince, goodnight indeed.

2015

Soon Enough

Jesus did not weep sufficiently. But that's the thing
with tears. They merely wet the cheeks, but
accomplish nothing. Take the vile taste from
your mouth, and breathe it in the air, to spread
like the stench of a corpse. In the night the
dead will visit you, and whisper: soon enough,
soon enough.
        The wind rips around the house,
a whisper, also a shout, rising almost
to words. I had rather the soothing sound
of wind in the trees, but the dark and cold
prohibit. So I lie under the thin covers.
My feet are cold, and the cold is rising
up my legs. Yes, there are visitors in
the night. I speak with them regularly now.

2016

Troll 1

I may not terrorize the night, or even
see it, so insular is this house. Its
chronic muteness. No lamp bides with my hand;
I cannot see, outside or in. The windows

are backed with silver, warding monsters dreamt
without, I suppose, but helpless to oppose
those within. It is a pale fishglow in the
darkness of a silent bedroom; swims the sea

of night, trolling for a hook, even at these
depths. I can sense the far-off sun, sparkling
on a surface that will never tell you anything
of what bides below. This kelp forest holds

me sleepless, hostage to the future.
Endlessly bemoaning a recriminant past.

2016

Falfurrias

At Falfurrias, there is a house with a shrine
in the yard. Our Lady of Guadalupe,
in concrete, draped in rock-hard muslin and blue, and
haloed with yellow stars; she blesses the grass burnt

yellow in the heat. They must paint the thing often
—the colors do not fade The artistry is
impeccable. I doubt the efficacy of
Portland cement in protecting anyone,

however. The statue provokes my unbelief.
I am so angered at the useless promises
of gods. As I pass, the sun pours down like honey.
You can see the yellow dust hanging in the blue
distance, like a muslin pall, and above that, in
the boil of white, so kind, the gentlest of brown eyes.

2016

The Old Way

My cousins lived in the old way. They'd a cistern,
and an outhouse. I awoke to the smear of
red light without the window, the shrill
annunciations of the rooster, the mild stench

of the chamber pot from the night just past. There is
dew and birdsong, and in the grass, I know the
ants scout for offal, as we might imagine the dead stir
in search of blood. The sun eats the dark; the clouds scud in

the spreading blaze of fiery light. There is a tumult
among the birds; they dive into the columns of
insects rising like smoke from the trees. The bats flee
to the place they were sent. If there was a god,

I would see him there, but he hasn't much
to do with the elderly stranger in the stories.

2016

The Splendid Stepchild

I am no hero in sheepskins, twirling my
Claymore like a baton. Them I love wear
the plumage of worms. There is grief in this for me.
Such the armor of dessication, the emollients
of decay. Evanescent, the mist has shifted.
Kings die, to whomever they might bring

gifts; neither St. George nor St. Andrew can
slay that green beast. I will ward the heart of my
mystery to the end. You will not pluck it out.
We knelt to Mithras with Constantine, but even
this did not kill the reptile. Still yet, they cast
that splendid stepchild aside. There is a style

and form to extinction. Gases and particulate,
shed like prayers, tend hopefully upward.

2017

The Bible According to Cecil B. DeMille

A cartoon cyclone of fire shoots fireballs at the rockface,
carving out commandments. Do that to the sinners,
my Sister always seemed to shriek. Don't waste it
on dead rock. Kill some sense into them. She'd rant,
her fond heart charred as any match, calling down not
the fires of hell, but those of heaven. She lived with God—.

But a God still crueler than that of Moses, God
according to Cecil B. DeMille. At the end, she
waited, speechless, as full of fear as anyone. I
miss her. She died like we all do: only that. Protection,
money, love—the largesse of her generous heart.
She had cared for us, expecting in return only utter and

complete obedience. She hated most everyone she
didn't know. She loved completely most everyone she did.

2017

Sedge and Bee

Anchor the fluent air in quartz shot with gold.
If an ardent heart smoldered on that altar, and
the sun, regardless of it, ran to seed, then
just as foretold, the weapons of prophecy,
of science, too, know that it was remorseless time,
hived in your head like honey, that brought you
low. There is no colossus to carry you
away, or revenant to keep you in your
grave, and although these are lessons refused
by most, once refused, all remain in that vague state
of curiosity, confounded utterly by
obdurate matter. *Ecce homo*, it is said.
Death is mere silence, the true, hard grip of
still more passing time. And of nothing at all.

2017

Mesquite

You can't kill them. You may root them out with fire
and claw, douse them with toxic waters, leave a
bulldozed waste in your wake—and here they come
again. A sturdy tree, but ugly, good to cook
with, useless for much else. They reflect somehow
like infinity in sheeted mirrors. The poorest
soil blossoms in sedge and bluebonnets, where
the limestone ledges root deep in the yellowed
hills, breaking out like the bones of giants. Cedar
spotted about. When the cock crowed, it did so from
just there. This place has made a nave of cruelty, as
high-toned as that. Mesquite, thorned, twists into the sky;
it is lain in the earth like the claws of a tumor.
But tear it out by its crowned roots, it will yet return.

2017

Fine Ruddy Pears

Cribbed pears do drip a morning sap, but this portends
naught but dissolution. Even sunrise will not
make a poem, unless the mind and ear consort.
The mind is like Anansi, black busybody,
scuttled out on impulse, of devils the cleverest;
the eye, buxom as foretold, brings to the bruising thing
only its own element, a thunderhead roiling
in the north, refuge of sinners, bearing down upon us.
The giant forced upwards, self-interest blunt as that
hammer, also foretold. This next martyr
to the gross cause, with black alacrity,
persevered on a set course no scruple could disrupt.
Images used, reused, borrowed, stolen, all to serve this
most merciless of masters, most servile of intentions.

2017

Sacrifice of the Periwinkles

And still there are those twisted trees. This my dream,
of periwinkles and apes alike? The thorns
won't spare you. Obey all orders of instinct
'till swept off-stage, and wrapped in linen. Notoriously.

Bourn up by the *deus ex machina* of active delusion.
For a moment, I thought all were saved. Then time
came slamming down like God's fist, the rush of hot
ash that seals up cities like pressed flowers.

Nor seemed deterred by that white rush, that would
deflower the stunned girl. A pregnant tumult
in midair. We can fill the voids, and conjure
up those final terrors with spells like plasters

of Paris. Do ill humors mask the whiteness?
A sacrifice, a meal, a torrent of carnal delight.

2017

Everything

The grackles crack their throats. They die in the
tree's roots, clawed feet so like human hands. As
the poets note, there is a pocket slum there of bright
blooms. What tumults despoil the ears of Satan? That
worthy serpent, coiled in the nest. The sky is
misapprehended. I am hunger-strung, and
anxious, just as she said it. Hard to slake, so
fitted is my form for black luck. All merit's
in being beef, but if spring is in fact like a girl
undressed, I'd only want to fuck her. Blood's broth
was filched by this hand. She has said it again. Though
prime parts cram each meal, the hunger remains,
a goad unto further rapine. I stand in the wrecked
kitchen. The world is mine to get everything wrong.

2017

Troll 2

He'll not scant his want until the larder is sacked.
This troll, with his oddball tonsure, will leave us
under the bridge bone-bare. In the still trenches of a

chilly five a.m., the colorless vacuum where smoky
dreams of blood and fire, too clear by far in the
ice-blue moonlight, face that ghost, the would-be-oracle
who will leech from us centuries of blood, make of us
slaves to golden wonders of incomparable
vulgarity, climax to gilded ages long past.

Can there be no Godly utterance, no potent
spell, no incantatory imprecation to intervene?
Telltale tatters at the outermost fringe of vision,
that rocky gizzard foretold of the earth. God may
know what is there to be chewed. But he isn't telling.

2017

He's the One Looking Outward

The Judas Goat leading us to slaughter glows orange
like a stellar carrot. Its round period, displacing
the next new moon's curve with curdled milk. Go, ghost of
our dreaming children, to the playground. The rising
waters give Dame Alice new context for critiques
of marriages as remote from her as she from us.

But the goat trod onward, the water its easy road.
Betrayal never sinks, but floats, ready like the freshest
turd, for aquatic adventure. There, in that cloud-
cuckoo land of colored wheels, we find the truth
of the cuckold. That keeper of truth waits in the
boat now himself, hanging from the naked rafters.

Hail and farewell, keeper of the timepiece, prisoner
of the profane grail, mouthpiece of the dreaming skull.

2017

Moment of Creation

Only the rich remember the past, supine on the board,
the condiments arrayed neatly—presentation—there,
where the spiders ate. They can gnaw it down
to a preferred shape, then come back in broad day

to the same place, the same face, the same brute mouth,
steady chewing, the same happy, unheroic past. An
amused shout from the Indians lined up for slaughter,
and turkey and a nice green bean casserole. "A miracle?

A miracle!" Arms outstretched to the absent deity.
That knocks me out. Do they touch the thing they see?
Feel the wind? Smell the dust? Though the bushes blooming,
bloom still in the oyster eye, never quite come alight.

Never quite afire. Never quite red. Never quite truly burning,
never quite itself, never quite anything, never quite anyone.

2017

Sonic Boom

Sweet blood, mouthfuls of it, shadows. And something
else. The spirit wakened in the night wind is naked,
but what hides within it? It thirsts less for blood,
than semen, more for that moment sweet as pain.

Bitter as the bit cheek's blood. What hauls me through
air—astride the broom, beneath the wings—I know
not, I only know I go on. Streaming long hair
behind, thighs clamped, shoulders flexed, mouth screaming

into the rush, while the sound tumbles from my heels
like a thunderclap. I am white as Godiva,
naked and willing, splayed feminine. It is
the man that takes life, squeezing it out by

the drop. I unpeel the dead hands, open the
dead eyes in the boiling white cauldron of morning.

2017

Mob of Owls

Hooves are hardened in the fleeing distance, while
from the head sprout horns to keep meekly the
mortal rendezvous. Here, in the black-twigged forest,
is a hand with which to pour the discontents
from your too-bitter heart, because it is bitter,
and because it is your heart. To fill it, bring teacups;
roll away all the aches. I will do whatever
you tell me. Will I marry you? Owls brood here on
mice murdered, shrews shredded; It is certain you
will thumb shut my eyes at the end, and dissolve
in sorrow. We make new stock from the salt. I notice.
I wait stark naked. All about this suite,
poison grows; in this fell dark, the water of tears
is black and stiff, but not at all that bad a fit.

2017

Omniscient Ignoramus

Logic and proportion have fallen sloppy dead.
Thorns and thistles were brought forth, thus to confound
me. I promised it. In the Nocturne, when Adam delved, Eve
span, and unto Adam it was said, because you have
eaten of the tree, the ground is cursed for your sake. It is
from such windy citherns of yore we convert omniscience
into ignorance. If we did agree in principle, I think,
still, nothing would be clear. But take a masque beyond the
planets, where bawdiness, unpurged by epitaph, may be
indulged at last, and you will find only airless ice,
comfortless, bodiless. The flagellants, well-stuffed, are less
disaffected than they feign. Smacking their muzzy bellies,
proud of such sublime proclivities, it was a hookah-smoking
caterpillar gave me the call—but oh, so many years ago.

2017

For Beth

It is a confusion of orange with gold, of
fruit with element, that has conjured up from the
granites of Manhattan this vulgarian palace,
painted with it thick. Why is it that I, a poor
man, can live gratefully, while this one is
mad in the service of his envy, and his wrath?

Are we not obliged always to remember what
the dormouse said? Palm to palm remains holy,
seeking the inward moistness. The white knight is
walking, at least; but in what direction, and towards
what is another thing. The Red King cries for my
head. I view his fear and lust, his sloth, and I am

afraid. I've known with you love warm enough
to prove flesh real. You are a gift. Thank you.

2017

The Untold Drowned

Out of the light evolved the morning as it
moved, as orchids float, in the swimming distance.
The morning summer did hue the deck,

where in that ambrosial latitude, limpid
waters lay rolling. They suggest the malice
in the millions of the untold, drowned, where
a loyal conjuration of clearing
opalescence in flat notes bespeaks, but will
not forgive the sea—that metamorphosis
of crystal blue and too-fluent green. In
rivers elsewhere, the water flows over

weeds that flatten in the direction of
the current, and the female, obscure,
fragrant and supple, conceals herself.

2017

Out in Rain and Back in Rain

Enormous undulations, fearful, flee
the broaching light, where, we are told, before, the
watchman passed on his beat. Out in rain, back in
rain, to cut water and fetch trees. Always

unwilling to explain. A rationalist, in a
tricorner hat, in a square room, disdaining
rhomboids and curlicues. He forgot that
love set us all going like watches. Then,

the clouds reflected a slow effacement
at the wind's hand. There are flickers among
the flat pink roses. I wake to listen, I stay
to learn, hungry for other than ignorance.

A far sea moves in my ear. Your handful
of notes: the clear vowels rise like smoke.

2017

Asylum, Brother

I reached the far shore of salt seas, but I dislike
nevertheless the ants crawling in and out
of my shadow. A bald cry took its place among
the elements; it magnified your arrival. Your nakedness

shadowed our safety. We stood around blank as walls.
All the knives of malice, the guns in the long streets,
show he was mistaken: the stars are so very distant. The
clouds distill mirrors, to reflect their own slow diminishment

at the hands of entropy. Of heaven, the antique reflection
rolled remorseless round and round those fleets of paper
boats. A moth-breath flickered among the buzzing
june bugs. She woke listening: one cry, and she stumbled

from bed, cow-heavy and floral. I mine her for blood.
Poetry is the babbling of the inmates, you know.

2017

A Mother's Secret

They were born near where Rome would be. Their
mother conceived them, she said, when Mars, always
the moral one, visited her in a sacred grove.

They were suckled by wolves. They descended from
nobility. And they said all that as if it mattered. But
what was it she hid there? So near the fluent air,

even anchored in amethyst, what could prevent
these two most perishable of brothers going
feral? The sky may be blue crystal streaked with rose,

but it was we, all loss, and its resistance, who
kindled the envy of angels and gods. The cock's
tail gleams in the sun. His feathers bluster and flare.

Romulus told of the founding. But there was
always the essential murder, with which it was begun.

2017

A Gray Promise

Silver petals of orchids, the prelude, whitened
far below. They moved in a swimming
green of watery radiance, while the
hues of the sea pour brilliant. The glistening

blue of ocean lay in sinister flatness. I
strode submerged in that malevolent sheen.
I saw the mortal massivenesss of blooms.
The instant flare of a future unmade

looks in askance your minuet, however
you may sweat to hold such darling wrecks
in your head. These crystalline pendentives, this
macabre water-gloom, that fetes the enormous

heaving of the planet. I have fled the slop of the
sea he knew, its gray promise of loss and sorrow.

2017

Dead Among the Pigeons

The power in the stories crackles along, killing
some, robbing others. The little deaths, where cringing
paramours, cow-eyed, suck the toes of the mighty.
I see Zeus among us, the muttering king, impotent

in his rage, at chastities unasked for, hot for the
promised coupling—a bull, a swan, the warm shower of
gold. The virginal blood commingles heavenward. Is this
some haunt of prophecy? The revenant chimera,
to suck the blood of innocence. But when he does,
whose imperishable bliss will that be? It has
been rightly said that rivers do seek for seas, but
it is the stars I stray among, impassioned with all

those potent spirits of yesterday. I do see God there,
dead among the pigeons, speckled and rank.

2017

The Surreptitious Blow

They gather in the waning day wing to wing
on the strung wires. On fences, the swags of
streetlamps and signal lights. Some Raptor of old

might climb from that soft and floating road through
darkness, lapping the blood of victims untold.
It's a steep ladder through all shifts of nature

to heaven, where the goatherd rises, and the
helmeted heads loom huge and cower lightly,
hands covering the lightless eyes, knees and feet

drawn tight. As if to receive a surreptitious
blow in the breadbox. Floats steadily upward,
in balance upon this incipient extinction, and at

length, like the bursting of lungs in the deep, breaks forth
on the air. Let us now praise famous men, indeed.

2017

How Better?

On the wet roads of autumn nights, they're gathered as the
light dies. Wrung out of this haven, yes, yet here,
of celebration and hysteria, there is nothing. How should we
know it? How should these poor parents so earnestly wish

us well, where, always suspect, their ignorance and skinned
sadness cannot but make harm? To find ourselves thus weakened.
Hurt internally. Already beyond all use of estimate, yet still
amenable, were it there, of goodness. Defenseless and

unknowing, without choice. Without knowledge for choice, if he
had it, while without power of choice if he had knowledge.
I have heard it. This revolution does take forever. No retreat,
only the uprooted, weeping, and human place in so

immane and outrageous, so wild and unfeeling a world.
How shall we do better than suggest a few possible laws?
And our fathers that begat us. As if they yet lived.

2017

Avis 1

Avis did everything—laundry, floors, dishes,
even windows. Her skin was a deep, glowing
black. Sometimes her skin flashed purple, too, despite
the plain wear and tear, as if reflecting from
some great depth. Quite lovely, even then, to me.
One day she told me to stop running in the house.
I said in reply, You can't order me around.
You work for us. She sulled up like a spring thunderhead,
clearly unhappy. Later, she and my father
were deeply in congress. My father glanced at me,
but Avis looked steadily in my father's
eyes. I did not worry. The next day, I ran
through the kitchen. She snatched me up and gave
the licking of all time with her hard, hard hand.

2017

An Infinite Talent

So much depended on that red wheelbarrow, in the rain.
In search of famous men to praise, I read of Paterson. Bad
TV and murder, where they shone on the glowing screen
in rhinestone and glitter. That left the perpwalk; the strut.

The housewives of carnage. I do yet recall the nation
they taught me of in school, the same schools graced
by that storied wheelbarrow. But at each iteration,
it was said, the little cut, cut clean, left a field where the

infinite talent for deceit could frolic with abandon, being of
as many kinds as this particular set of senses could receive
and reflect upon. Perhaps, at a time, we did carve strictures
of light, did punch steep holes in the gliding heavens, step

measurements precisely upon some grand estate of being. But
that was in some other country. And besides, the wench is dead.

2017

Lost Vehemence

Here, again, in the midst of all these, is this human
creature born, awaiting that touch of the divine
that never comes. Shrunk up to meat merely,

weakest of all these instruments, its taking titanic
nevertheless, beyond exhaustion, infinitely beyond
all we receive, a daily bread sacred beyond our recognition.

Held in that blurry space between motive and volition.
Planted nevertheless, and continuously, in the
blood's deep, it holds. It holds—each slashes its mark, yet
not one negligible: and they measure, not only by
multitudes but within each granular instant. Might I yet
whip up my flagging strength, forget all kindnesses,

recover that youthful radiance, naked and aroused? Feel
yet again that lost vehemence of midnight and bedsheets.

2017

Monsters

Reflect upon the physical; consider the mind.
Emotions and economics, the mental, the
glandular, the medical predicament of habit
and belief.
           The complex interlock and interform,
that conspires in a companionship still sharper, fiercer,
stricter. All the more bonebiting traps and equations

of destruction than are in the power of any
one or five or ten of us independent; until
one night a pale silver blotch along the floor saw
petals of white roses unfolding to my touch.

Broach the milk in that with the saltiest purge. Do you
hear the sea unfolding in the bedclothes? They had as
well be the coffins hid in the shrunken tundra of arctic
islands, the grinning, heavy-lidded monsters within.

2017

Perfect Indolence

Deluded with sapphired ice, what good is a drafty
museum? Your nakedness shadows a dead lust. The cloud
that distills a mirror to reflect its own slow dripping
is like the patterns of damasks that were shaken off

from the loosed girdles in the spangled gloaming, the sighs
and whispers of penetration, as the more suddenly
heaven roiled, and the day came, blowing and voluble.
Good clown. There ought to be more of them. One thought

of British chocolate, and large umbrellas on a wet street,
and a motley green of untrimmed lawn. If you follow the
drift of the obese machine, perfected in indolence,
ingenious and droll, you might, too, have beheld the

sovereign clouds as jugglery. See them watching wide
-eyed? Their mouths are open, clean as that same cat's.

2017

Audacious Decadence

America is long since settled in the mold of its vulgarity.
There can be no such thing as too much, we said. The flower
fades to make fruit, yes, and the fruit rots to make earth. The
swirl and ache from sprays of honeysuckle, suckled like

mother's breast, is not too much. But for us, the flow of some
other milk, from hidden springs in the deep gloaming, brought
the craving for the sting of pepper, it is true. For the
strong sweets. Too long thickened into empire, corruption

may not be compulsory, but the cities lay at the monster's
feet, and in the mountains now, the woods, ripeness and
decadence compete to build all the higher. All the more
audacious. That was the trap that caught the noblest. Death

blameworthy nevertheless, being death, and the mortal
remains splendid despite themselves. Yet still, do keep a distance.

2017

The Republic

Dashed with that pain, it all not only lacks
salt, but there is no burning clove nor bitter
bark I will not swallow down. We stood up
to the sky, but only to break. The petal of
the rose stung, too. Its sweetness all the
sweeter for it. It was the butcher's hand, the
fool atop the mountain, lord of the thickening
center, who squeezed blood from the stones.

Now, no mark of sand or rock can reach this bone,
too long enfolded, in too much flesh. The blood of
the mind drips yet, dreams of murder, lusts for
rapine. The Republic perishes, in the throes of its

deepest vulgarity. All we have left is the insufferable,
and God never walked the earth at all.

2017

Dervishes

When it comes for me, it will be the owl-eyes in the
scraggly woods, saucer-wide and oyster-white. Twin
handymen, well-armed with tools, lethal and gleaming,
the better to rip out those inward organs where the pretty
tunes were played. I will be in bed, perhaps alone, perhaps
not, some screed gripped in my hand as I puzzle out
the crawling insects all in a line. It always seemed
so neat, yet convulsions of thought swirled within it
like gyres, like whirlpools. The ants carried off the
tiny wet chunks, the better to swell their larder.
Mother is frightened, and the dogs cringe and whine.
It isn't the farmboy alone who turned wolfish.
May poets to come see, too, that dervish of swirling dark
and light I could never fathom, but never escape.

2018

Hang Fire

The sky that was once so deep, beyond blue
in its depths, is known now to be shallow
as a tear. Yet we go on, as if declining
to surrender mattered somewhere, somehow
within this vast and inconsolable scene.

I've seen cloudscapes like fairylands, forests
like cathedrals, seas of aquamarine and
amethyst. But now, I am strangely unmoved.
In some dry gulch near Midland, I choked on

oil and sand, while the relentless,
oscillating hum of the wind turbines
ground me to dust. Virtue is lost on me.

Vice is beyond my doing, and relentless
myself, I hang fire, alive beyond all sense.

2018

Gun Cotton and Fresh Shit

Seven soldiers in a line fire three times. There is the flag, folded
perfectly, for the wife, the mother of his children. He
is gaudily deceased, after three wars and one fitful peace, here
in the precincts of respectable death. The soldier.

Reduced to a pale nose, just visible beyond the rim
of the coffin. It seems parsimonious. Cheese-paring,
like the proctor of a government project. A factotum
counting of beans in a budget. I know that exchange exists.

Greed rules, selfish motives abound. We preach generosity, but
practice something quite different, and so much more cruel.
The coffin is built like a sports car, chrome and primary colors,
roaring off, utterly masculine, into eternity. With a noisy

roar and a squeal, and a cloud equal parts burnt fuel and rubber.
His reality was less so, and smelt of gun cotton and fresh shit.

2018

The Irradiated Dark

We carried her foot and shoulder into
the garage, secret and dark. Bare studs over tar
paper, dusty jars of nails, cobwebs, a box
of tools, strange machinery to be put to

obscure purpose. She was crying out, begging
to be let off, I think. But once secreted thus,
we stripped her dress and blouse, and beheld that
mysterious mound of cleft flesh, conundrum

of unease and obsession. This was followed soon
enough with adolescent grapplings in the irradiated
dark. It was never startlingly original or striking.
Ordinary lust directed at ordinary girls.

Doom boiling ominously to east and west alike, while
the future held the waxlike bodies and the dry blood.

2018

Trifles

It all begins innocently enough. And then,
a fight blossoms from nothing, and penny
ante stakes balloon into apocalyptic tremors.
It is in the absurdity of marriage and other sorts

of those least ad hoc of relationships to turn
on a trifle. But a mad fuck on the spur
of a vanishing moment is among
the most rational of things, all open

wet mouths and engorged flesh and the voiding
out of fluids. God damn it. I'm too old
to be reasonable and still too young
to be wise. Move aside all devils, all angels;

there are souls to crush and hearts to break.
And who has anything at all, if it is not words?

2019

A Clutter of Knives

I remember my mother wringing laundry, sturdy
and implacable. She wore a white dress, red
roses tumbling all down. Her short hair was dark.
Sweet things, too, are lost violently. We happily
squander all. I tried it in other places, equally
paradisical. Somehow, a vital spark was missing.
I came home to Texas. Cruel from the beginning. Anglo
and Hispanic alike in this, sharpening their guile on

one another, and on the chattel blacks. There was
air to breathe again. So strangely enough, I prefer
to live where I'm alive. The past and its sorrows
like mud to be trudged through, in heavy black rubber

boots. A walk barefoot in the grass appeals. Yet outside, it
is winter yet, and the grass like a clutter of knives.

2019

The Boundless Thing

A sliver of light spills out, yellow and
glowing. Without which tulips may not grow,
the death in the other room be no more than
a distant echo of those others, long dead.

Impermanent masters of that infamous
plot of land encompassing the unquiet dead.
Barely large enough, we're told. Human folly
remains the one truly boundless human thing.

We keep it in an oblong box, at a sharp
angle from the front door. Just open a crack.
Return constantly to the news feed, waiting for
the end of the world to drop from the sky.

Doomed, blaspheming roundly, the long, dull
fall from one sort of foolishness to the next.

2019

Quiet At Last

The old man, ungently drunk, floats a foot
or two above his insecurities. My mother,
in the kitchen, awaits his attention.
He moves on her like an army. A stride

filled with resolution. My brother and I
weep beneath the dining room table. We have
there the sugar bowl, incongruous, out of place.
Daddy is not tall. He does not tower over her,

as she reaches into a drawer and comes out
with the butcher knife, mundane. Everyday. Commonplace.
Lay a hand on me, she says. I'll spit you like a chicken.
Waiting for the other bomb to drop,

my brother and I eat sugar, spoon upon spoon.
She is quiet at last with her mouth full of blood.

2019

The Trembling of Grief

I wish I could say something good about
my family, the long years when I was so
little, so fugitive from adult passions. Something

that would make a kind of sense. Parties,
excursions, vacations, beloved toys—all
blotted out. Hiding under furniture

was a thing. We did it often. The sounds
of violent lovemaking were a thing,
too, though this we would understand only

later on. A mouth full of blood was not
enough. It must dribble and drip. There must
be screams, and imprecations. Suffering

must be held in the hand, cupped with the
heart's blood, where it might tremble for a time.

2019

He Saw the Bread Baked

So el Diablo's on his coffee break, contemplating all
those years. The steady grapplings with fellow merchantmen
and stevedores of like exotic tastes. The crystal beasts still
yet on the knick-knack shelf. No more could he

escape the toils of aberration than the mighty hunter,
killer of lions, builder of walls. To be sure, also
the friend and companion of scorpions. Lover and patron
of tavern wenches, who saw the bread baked all those days.

A continuum from here to decay. But death is such an
orderly thing. It's true. Gilgamesh had his lovers, he had
his joys, he dwelt in a nether sadness, as must we all. Where
was Enkidu then? Fucking a whore or chasing a gazelle?

How much do you rely on friendship? How much on tyrant
time? It all fades, and quickly, too, into the encroaching dark.

2019

He Might Have Lived

Bitterness at times is just too cloying sweet,
flavor notes struck back of the mouth, in the
sinuses too, too flavorful; better the
sharper sting of forgiveness, a blood taste on

the tongue. Who among us does not require it?
All our yesterdays light one fool only the
way, not per se well,
                              but too, too wisely.
My discontents winter in Aruba, along with

the money. All history discernible there
and elsewhere, A face, an unguarded word,
a wound. Who does not die alone? Even if
someone is there, they aren't apt to go with

you willingly. Are they? To the betterment
of the locals, when he might have lived to be old.

2019

Light Aslant

The light comes into it aslant the darkness, as of
a window, while a mist as of clouds hangs, up there,
distant amid the trusses. The world entire, the flesh
entirely beyond the world, tumescent in
our death-obsessed dreaming. God is busy
elsewhere, if you believe that; the world itself

his oyster, where it burns stark mad. No more
than one enormous room. It is mad while it
is blissful, this warm stench of fevered flesh.
Like sweet grain of early summer, inexplicably
soured in the silo. Here there is no beauty,
no love, no silence, no ugliness, and no shout that

has not its use. The penultimate gesture is the
bored yawning mouth, always open for business.

2019

Claiming Territory

It just precedes the louder voices, ecstatic or fearful,
as may be. Ever content with its rapaciousness,
there is still the birdsong in the staking of a
territorial claim. Was this the tale foretold?

Or of some other, if similarly atrocious get?
Glad at the poetic gloss, we may say, but
bright feathers are no prelude to a fucking,
bad or good. And isn't it just that selective.

Blindness we delegate to the god, in the precincts
of uncertainty, just so the time will smoothly pass.
A brief moment of thoughtful, silent sanity, quickly
gone. As he himself, what gives us these troubles?

Do not go gentle into anything, young fool; but grab it
by the ears, and give it the wettest, deepest kiss.

2019

She Was Not the Last

My father died when I was sixteen. Shrunk to a
scarred face, a cheap blazer, black slacks. The Masons
in their aprons joked among themselves. My brother
died when we were in our forties. He went hard,

convulsed amid the disordered sheets. The big decision was
whether to drug him, so he would be less upsetting
while he died; crock him to the gills and while waiting, talk of
other things. In the end, we did that. Debate to the

rhythm of Cheyne-Stokes breathing. That terrible silence,
in which we spoke faster and louder, wondering when
and if the next breath would come. When he died at last,
my mother wept so. Inconsolable. There were red roses

on the table top, such as my father had loved. They withered all
when my mother died. And strangely, for she was not the last.

2019

Haute Coture

The hospice worker propped her up in her bed like
a mannequin. She grasped in one hand a rosary, such
as she seldom if ever used, though she did often
declaim loudly and at length her proud subservience
to God, the father, the tormentor, the executioner,
and she would have said it dead and all, growing colder
by the second, her eyes lidded and her cheeks sunk,
her lips parted on her teeth, in all the rictus of
the forever-waiting grin, forever unlooked for,
looking less like herself than the model of a skull, set
up somewhere for the schooling of children. But she was
dead. Thus down the runway; here, ladies and gentleman,
is death, the last word in haute couture. Ambitious and
unambitious alike, a long life and a short drop breed silence.

2019

An Equality

I must have written her a thousand poems, each dripping
with more adulation than the last. There was no
past, and certainly no future. Never discussion
of whence we might go, or when, or what the fate of
our respective children might be. I held some vague notion
that she would be a mother to mine, but she was mother
already, hostage to hearts of equal flesh, equal blood,
and forever and always in all things equally bruised.
Nor was there talk of our own fates, as if none was
there to be lived. Only single moments, a hot
breath of mutually insatiable desire, held in
a cusp of time. On her back, with her breasts smiling
upward, begging the touch of hand, lips, tongue. The
moment when the legs open to the moist, warm inwardness

2019

The Upside of Gaza

Her eyes do gaze, but they do not see. This
is not to be controlled. Unseen is not
unremembered. A room, the proverbed nutshell.
The slow, ungentle fading has come at last
to this, dead lights in a deep place. Glints at some
indefinite distance, an improbable

remove, an undeserved fate. Visits from
relatives so frequent before, reaching some
sort of peak in the near past, but here now, lost
in the dark that swallows it, neither to be
heard nor seen again. There are worse horrors,
painted in another color than red.

But she remembers red. She remembers it
when she rails inwardly at such a fate.

2019

At Home with the Warrior

His was a war in a heated place. Strange that he talked
most of the temperature, the steaming paddies, and how
cool it became when they rode the choppers.
He came home thin as the proverbed rail, his dress greens
hanging from his shoulders, not a flag of defeat, but
a banner of narrow escapes. He might romp his Charger
out of Piggly Wiggly, the rear end skittering side to
side, and smoke blowing black from the shrieking tires.
His wife,my cousin, terrified in the front, clung
to him, while I clung for dear life to a seatbelt,
cowering in the back. He took up those other choppers,
too, right away. It was as if he would hew to that
very narrowness. As if he would give it the most
devouring kiss. As if he loved it dearly as a woman.

2020

A Piece of Work

Why do you weep, hired man? That's all of us. That's
all of you. Embarrassments of lethal moment,
a scowling Danish prince's black shadow, his bad
teeth. Such poor forked beasts as we, wretched boy.
And what is it you worry so in your mouth? Shout it
out into any old wormhole.
      No whisper
to disturb this silence. What events, perceived on
the cheap, lie beyond this horizon now?
They will stay 'til you come. I promise; watch that
long, scudding shadow of a cloud. See if it
hits the moon. Whip and flail, sedge and bee. What a
piece of work is man.
      This endless, pining, insane
melee, of compassion, sorrow, grief.
What need of a reason? Dead, was all he said.

2020

How Droll I Was

All history figured in one betrayal.
Less grand than Iago, but grander still than Judas,
that cauldron of iniquity. She teeters all
the while on the brink of extinction, insanely
beautiful, and everywhere, the vilest hint of
mild death. Who would glorify those immemorial
indifferences?
                That skull grins for a reason. It
is a good joke, this unflinching, row on row
mendacity of clueless, graceless men, lying
about their conquests. It ever struck me how softly
women can peel away from raging, rigid
desire. How cruel.
                How droll I was. So caught
up in self absorption, the sharp bite of forgiveness
stinging the tongue, the blood taste of slow time.

2024

Texas

I was maybe six, at the Stockyards, and someone
calls out, "Will you sell me a tamale, Pedro?"
Insults are exchanged, invitations are issued
to Remember the Alamo. Remember Goliad.

Remember the fucking Maine. Incomprehensibly,
it goes that way. Unmistakably pointed and obscene
provocations and retorts. Gringo. Spic. Triggers
—oh we do all so love them all, especially

when followed by a bang. So bloody a history.
So much of it. Factors of theft, abuse, war, and
plain old murder. There was no way a boy child
could not learn about guns. A random pleasantry

might be, "Can I fuck your sister?" How did, "Why can't we
just get along?" ever become such a stupid thing to say?

2024

The Anguished Glance

We are all dying, only at different
speeds. One may wear some better than another,
capable of the same labors at the same
pace a longer while, but it will set in;
everyone wears. And everyone wears
out. I remember the first dead person
I ever beheld. Not merely saw. My
grandfather, and my Aunt Vera weeping
in the background saying over and over,
Damn you Daddy. Damn you Daddy. And I,
a small child only, asked, Can I touch him?
My mother, an anguished glance at her sister, said,
Yes. And so I did. And he was so very cold.

2024

Avis 2

So, Avis came to our house once a week to clean.
She did all that stuff. Mom was working already;
it was a big help. Sometimes my father
drove her home, over near Hattie Street, he said.
One day he came home smiling like a spotlight.
He clomped through the house. His workboots boomed like
doom on the pier-and-beam and the hardwood.
We could hear him and mom yammering in their
bedroom, then laughing, then a serious tone.
Daddy came finally back to the front, to tell us.

Avis introduced me to her children. She got them
all out of the house and lined them up like soldiers.
There were nine of them, all yes sir and no ma'am.
They looked as if they should have rifles at port arms.

2024

An Eye for an Eye

More often it is some person that is the get of a flooded soul.
The waters rushing down a pretty girl's face, an
old man's remembrance of passion. The bubble on the far
horizon is certainly a wave, and whence it came I

cannot say. When the nails are pulled the bodies fall with a thump.
No serenade of shrieks this time—he's dead.
Be kind, I beg you, be kind; there are musty exhalations
of rooms abandoned to dust and spider webs. Say

what you will do, do what you want. You need, like Jesus,
the protocols of dying well. Some new and clever
Neverland garlanded with Dragon Lillies, that smell just like a
corpse. Renders down to history, all death and bloodshed, too,

into a sort of gluey mass stuck on the shoe of a grim old man,
who is dressed in a way very much like an executioner

2024

Overtly Political

Did you buy one of those goddamn guns?
I know, I did. It's like hiring a whore,
isn't it? Short and sleek and easy to point,
and the clip full of that NATO five-five-six.
I bought two extra banana clips. Man, I
could shoot up a school with one of those, but
now. If anyone ever tries to shoot up
our school, I'll just blow them half in two. One
burst, viscera everywhere. Fucking libtards.
They think of a world devoid of bloodshed,
free of strife. What the fuck.
It's good we have truly fine citizens,
who buy with an eye to future malice,
and to kill one of them fools now and then.

2024

Hunted

Crescendos in the flesh, flowers in flame—
how much we change. How much we do not change.
Here was the passage of a great Beast through
a narrow place. So much we change. So much we

have changed. Sonorous plain songs tell that once
upon a time there was this thing, the hunter,
with teeth like butcher knives and
once there was a singer who sang fearlessly.

They met one night so late, almost too late,
and discovered all unbeknownst what could
be taught and what could be learned; how much we
do, how much we do not. Where does one leave off

and the other begin? Death sought purposely, or
death by misadventure? All of that, in the end.

2024

The Bridge

Time drips down like water off a rail, right off
the bottom. There is the distant squalling of
a siren, the dialectic of a solitary grief,
as if an untimely declension of an almost
obsolete noun. The cars move quickly past the
flickering lights, that reflect on the dirty white
of the road snow; the body lay sprawled in the
steady brights of the squad car, and just then,

the ambulance showed, siren shrieking into
cold air. The entire tableau drew the stares of
carsfull of wretched, idle people, ogling
the bare feet of the body in the lights. He lays
as he fell. Down from the high bridge. Was that his
purpose going there? To a road to another road?

2024

Deceitful

An obsession endlessly discoverable, she
perhaps is more aligned with the dark than ought be.
You'd never make any wall in any bed clothes there,
but still yearn for it to pass on one eye to another,

ever watchful, when another is sleeping.
Kiss around the softness of those lips, and watch
the fall and rise of breasts under tented covers.
I think this lover is mine, yet I already seek

another. And if I lack sleep in watching the creep
of light from foot to head of her in the growing clarity
of her deep beauty, here in our house, our
room, our window, our bed. My thoughts of leaving

her vagrant at the threshold, discarded heart, quite
beyond both. And now, this deceitful sun finds me just so.

2024

That Which Arrives

That which arrives, both early and dearly, rather
than departing posthaste, does not fit. Achilles
has a Glock; he's gunning down sissies left
and right. Oh, I had to repair my own cars.

All my cousins told me so. Must trek into
the woods and kill things of fur and feathers,
lest the other boys think me strange. Hut one
two. Hercules on the Gridiron. It is true

I did not enjoy these things, yet I did them,
saddened by the dead bird, the stuffed stiffness
and still glass eyes of squirrels trophied on a bookshelf,
wired to a dead branch on a wooden base. How

could anyone not look at it and think:
That thing is dead, go now and bury it.

2025

Stonewall Fucking Jackson

Must fight. Beat with my balled fists all who oppose
me. Must not back down. Ever. Especially
when I am wrong, especially when I know it.

But why why why? Parents of my parents
haunt me. Cain and Abel in Conestoga
wagons,Yankees from Illinois, come into

north Texas to ally with the old rebels,
together kill off Mex and Comanch—
the other one among the Scotch-Irish

minions, babies and possessions all in
the wagon, all the long way from Alabama—
you others stand aside, we are the righteous
ones—Remember the Alamo. Remember
the Maine. Remember Stonewall fucking Jackson.

2025

Fableaux

Zoiks and zooks. God's blood. His squirming flesh, too;
he lied when he said he was willing, but who ever is?
We're all god damn cowards at the end.
At the end we are all roaring heroes.

The waif is a naif and the alleyways are ripe with
ambuscadoes, peeking over a boulder with his
arquebus. Match smoldering. Primitive fire.
Is not all violence primitive? Is it not bereft all?

Even that which devours whole cities. I remember
the B-58s out of Carswell; the flight pattern came low
over our house. The windows rattled in their frames,
the roar of the enormous engines so

near. End-times in themselves, I thought.
This world. Be patient, though. It will get worse.

2025

Games You Might Win

Weather curdling in the sky blue-black,
a frozen riot. Fallen all, with such
a disgraceful crash. Scurry like fleas in
fur. A ferris wheel we tumble off of
at the top, no impact. A merry-go
round that launches at escape velocity,

no lift-off, mere falling. Always rolling
down, no impact. Games you might win, but can't,
prizes you might take, but won't, and everywhere,
the sure-footed tumble of the gymnast shod
with lead. My discontents winter in Aruba,
along with the money. All history there.

To the happy betterment of all, gravity
wins. But he ought to have lived to be old.

2025

Benign Proclivities

Where it went too slow, now it will go too fast.
My heart a ragged vagrant, whispering formless
sorrows into its empty cup. She was swaying
over me silent, until I saw her; I whispered
to her, she is burst in Springtime, a special topography
of fools. The outlandish, crumpled shapes of clothing,
and bedspreads, the circling overhead fan wears over
our heads in endless circles. Is this less a thing
between us than a point of contact? With the closing of
a circuit. I love the way you fill me up, she says. And I
fill her up. There is something there of light and dark,
of mystery, and, too, the mundane. As old as the dark
in the hidden space behind my eyes. No appropriate
capital to span the pediment. But wait for it
—some forthcoming bewilderment more profound.

2025

Clytemnestra

I must tell you, tell you all that I have, all that I remember,
there is no other way. That it not be lost, to time
and nothingness. Mourning becomes the Easter bunny,
pink and fluffy. Love and avarice tumbled Corinth

down into tears and blood. Her way of coping, you see,
with the singular unpleasantness that stood out from
her history of penance for the crimes of more than
one other. For the bloody deeds of Agamemnon,

Aegisthus, and Clytemnestra, too. Not so different
from other crimes at other times and places; her own
transgressions, by the way, or by what light she had, that
might have been not much, but after all, was hers. Not crime

so much as justice, to her mind. That yawning red trap.
I beg you. Do but stay the awful hand that swats her.

2025

Inbred

As her daughter with her brother. Both of them doubly
bound. A crime to avenge a crime. Justice, that bitch dog,
sockets oozing puss and breeding flies, wrapped in a
filthy rag, clutched her scale; and a mercy unto herself

that she rather more than not deserved; but morning became
her. Not then not later, did she feel like a teacher,
fed on dark turgid wells of hatred, THIS PLACE ACCURST

the sign read, a darkness self-willed and self-orchestrated,
black and sweet. Who is not the victim of force more potent,
and with the greater malice? No longer in Gaza, eyeless.

I'll not break your statute, but he fell from the bridge. The car
struck ground and bounced and then shattering into a thousand
glittering shards as the windshield parted before his rush toward
death. They found his shoes in the floorboard, perfect and new.

2025

Crosstime Traffic

Hellishly protracted, infernal multiplications of time will not
bar you, exactly, from these smooth, efficient
matters, though the blissful ignorance of specifically carnal
knowledge might. If you permit the wheel to stay unmolested
at the top, the new circle the beginning of the old, you must
recall, that wheel was as tall as the top of the world; if only
it would've left us there, always beginning, always ending.
And my God, she was a beauty. Could I still, even if she were
seized by this Pharaoh, who would search out the borders of an
endless desert. Solomon knew that I didn't need to send to
ask; he *must* leave her undefiled, that I might defile her.
My grief runs out salt tears, a silvery, monochromatic sorrow.
The Little Death takes me, a lost time between prayers. Solemn
children await the ice cream truck; traffic is a riot in the ears.

2025

Bitterness

Spring came. It stayed awhile. Summer followed.
Things happen that way. With promises of
fleshy fulfillment, of the things that do
not change. But winter is still all the same for
these.
       No segue into barrens, but the promise
of barrenness itself. Shards of ice like razors,
limitless; bloodless quite before us, as
we dabble in the politics of passion, but
that's a misnomer; which part is missed? I'll be
the fly in the ointment; the Spider dangled
by the lampshade above your marriage bed,
sharp of fang and furrred of foot; I'll whisper excerpts

from the *Roman de la Rose,* while you hang fire,
and anyone's breast laid bare is an open wound

2025

Grief and Avarice

The blood boiling prairie, the debonair disarray
of the violently dead. My love is Scarlett,
standing over Tara, full of grief and avarice.
The whining bitch stole my book of love
poems. I've read each one by one. Before, I
wished I'd written every one to read to you, but
don't, since I didn't. Your least affection sucks
like a black vacuum, until nothing is left.
The infamous *Code Duello* avoids the more
dubious terms of engagement, each moment
flung on from there; I have no feelings deeper
than those I've read about. Just don't mind me;
I'm a harlequin, who has no feelings
deeper, really. Than his own climax.

2025

Athena in a Cypress

The green eyes loomed, imminent and disastrous
The words came tumbling out of you like brick
bats; what a healthy but pleasing idolatry.
We tell ourselves so many lies in the confusion,
that they cross like electric currents sparking and
spitting. Shrieks like a tree cut down; like a bitch dog,
fat with milk. Topless Athena, owl-eyed and cleverish,
sits in the branches of a Cypress and sings the song, not
sweet, but very wise. Less than more enraptured in my
eyes. What she takes when her sister gets her thing.
Thus Aphrodite rises soft on her half shell, and she
is one I know already, if too well. I sing a carcass;
can you afford a spit? Fiddle and moan and sit, more than
half mad, if little more than a quarter glad, baying at the Moon.

2025

Caving In

I am consumed with helpless, elemental
love. These smooth faces, these bright and clear eyes,
too intent on that cannibal feast, deliciously vile,
to note well the odds. A splatter of blood; an

ardent heart, a burnt offering smolders
on the altar. Someone slams the door and
crafty, hides the key in the cloakroom with
the cloaks. Should we somehow compromise?
Your study pulls you, but I'd ask that you remember,
and not be so annoyed that it's only the sound of
someone being born. Or dying. We grow bored with atrocity;
cruelties are banal. God forbid we miss anything on
TV. Time, that epic tyrant, grief and loss and plain death,
its endless careening fall into the past. The world is lost to us.

2025

Carnal Knowledge

And the universe contracted down to a point,
somewhere in the region of the navel. Then I
was as much of flesh as any living thing will
ever be, and still part of a woman's soul, because:
I loved her. I loved her body because I love that, too.
For mercy, let me tell you, that it not be lost.
Since yesterday's gone past saving, and tomorrow
never comes, you know what awaits us outside,
the children and the husband of the bride. Blissful
ignorance bespeaks a carnal knowledge that never
was, or only a few times. Yet all parties occupy
proper space in the universe now. Love's dog,
scratching fleas that bite and scamper and squirm
beneath the coarse, greasy hair, blood simple, blood fresh.

2025

Certainty

As if no other feeling were there. Just one
other beef, to be butchered and tenderized
for barbecue, head ablaze with mutually redundant
heat, a perch upon which death, tragedy, sorrow

of all makes and manufactures may safely be mocked.
Explosive instantaneous release. I scald you
inside, you burn me clean inside, and we rest
entangled, and gather strength to start the whole

process over again. Trapped in time, trapped in the
peeling meat. Whatever joke the times in flux may play,
my rapt devotion, the mud-like tug of growing,
certainty has no role in it. The artifice of love,

the craft of healing, in such an ardent tangle of
earnest hearts. There is no charm to lay the demons.

2025

Marionettes

The hall of mirrors in your eyes daunts me.
It's dark there, yes; and you the only light.
Even in the cold, spiders scuttle like
old people, across the mossy cobbles
and down, going somewhere. I'm not. Floating
in water curlicued with oily rainbows.
Get the cleaning supplies. Rinse, scrub well. Rinse,
scrub well. The mundane, mud-like tug, of
groceries not yet bought natter me like
bills yet unpaid. The children perform recitals
to a rapt audience. Troops of mimes in
motley, a solitary harlequin. A brief
tragedy of marionettes, arch as spiders.
There's nothing worse than remembrance.

2025

Compline

All that vulcanistic convulsion,
with which Spike Yahweh, that God serene and
laughing, not so long on silence as
other gods I know, beat us to the retort.

Millions died while he leered down from his
mountain top, still hungry for the brass taste
and iron smell of spilled blood, those inexplicable
roses splattered so widely. It is a dicey

thing to offend a prophet, much less a god.
But before its cage is breached—one more of
this maddening god's little jokes—think to
consider it a form of assay, to

separate the ore from the dross. Some of
those deities are also great with computers.

2025

The Box

What salvage of love, of grief can be made?
That old woman, enrobed in black and endless
patience, disposes us all. It is, after all,
an infinitely discoverable

universe. I don't know what I think
today. I don't know the times. I don't know
what I feel at all. I am the strong box of
myself; I am spent searching for the key.
Pandora made such effort for another
kind of box, but then she had less joy of
all she found than she expected; I knew
about that. I knew, too, either search as long

as there is to search for the key, or live in the
box. But I had rather live in the world.

2025

Now and Then

I can write no alba, no song of the
sunrise bright on the white of your arm; dappling
shadows of leaves in chiaroscuro, on the lines
of your face. I could have loved you once.

Did I? But here's now, and that was then.
It hasn't come about again. And if it
should, then knotted by some vagrant wind,
like always, shy of the mark. Always a

little bit stupid. I have no wit to do
justice to anything. Somewhere remote,
my pillow torments me. Your ghost breathes from it
remnants of perfume, and I awake with perfect

knowledge of what was, and what is. Perfect
your ignorance, stupid girl, of what was never.

2025

A Too-full Heart

The hunt is up, and the transplant after all
proceeds. Take my too-full heart, shredded
slowly, eaten by time, by malice to
a hollow, blackrich ruin; it wants its

pulsing drumbeat. I bury my face where your
head was lain. In that deep breath, time will pass.
Remnants ghost dance in shadow, the glaze of
elf light; medieval torments listed the

size of phone books, enacted in the head.
Move on, move on my green and lovely child;
That the hands of clocks do move is a bitter
pill, I know. An unplacated sun continues

prescribing its arc above all; not even the
fattest Tuesday can help that vagrant murder.

2025

A Moot Point

They may not find us asleep like spoons in a
drawer, yet something remains to sing of you
in a song. Even the worms in the apples
of our eyes respond well enough to lullabyes;
perhaps a baroque and protracted fashion
of saying goodnight, yet noise helps everyone
sleep. We all behave as if someone has died,
when really, who died, and when, is moot. A

grimness of purpose, perhaps in the act of
living. We twirl about in kissing circles,
intent on taking that ring, that isn't gold,
yet on we go, like dervishes, seek that ecstatic
union; bloom of a certain flower leaves its nude
husk to tatter; a fragile skull merely waits to die.

2025

The Bethlehem Game

The most fragile game is madness. The faster
we go the slower the resolution; still yet
do I shed tears. Am I altogether a history
of flood tides? Nothing that I can see slouches

any nearer Bethlehem, to be born or to die. If
there is a wisdom in tears, it must be waters
of another place than Babylon, crowded so near
the river, bitter with salt and iron. Tears

shed in the dark are a lesser thing. Is it a
matter of choice, as the Overseer claims? What type
of exile after all, flesh of your flesh, the endless
corrosion of endless grief. I know too well

of tears not shed, and startled from my stony
sleep, I know too, not but I can stand.

2025

Orestes' Solace

There is no solace in the hand that strokes, nor
the more clogged the throat, with all the words piled
up, bestowed as you yourself saw fit, he
said. Air quotes, air quotes. It was I who did these

things, no prince, nor much less god. The two ends
of a string was what tamed them, finally. Gods came
to them, transformed them to benign givers of counsel,
if not in Corinth, then elsewhere, since there are

many Gardens in the world, and many oases
and many forests and deserts and seas. That
done to spite all the dying, all the weird stuff
bypassed in the night, I spent my own time nailed,

arms stretched, convulsed with the horrid struggle to exhale,
like a whiner deluxe, all the tomorrows of my yesterdays.

2025

Mourning Becomes Us

One rosey burst of light, that they greet with planchant
cries for more, and watch it all bespread some vagrant
collection of vapors, with something like rapture;
all that, when he knew that what waited, curious
across the river, all tooth and claw, was poised to rip.
Oh, my precious legroom, of what sweetness you're made.

Electra was a night person, very fond of bar hopping
and one night stands. This her way of coping, you see,
with all the singular unpleasantness that stood
out from her history. Appearances for crimes.
Matters of more than one other, for the bloody deeds
of Agamemnon, say. Or Clytemnestra, Mommie

dearest. Mourning had arrived indeed. When they patiently
bore whatever stripes that grinning hag saw fit to inflict

2025

That Bed

Everyone should make love once at least in a four
poster bed. I remember us like that. You weren't
on top, yet I sat up, still inside you. Your breasts
were at face level, round white decanters, from which
I took long drinks, and then went over with you and down
over the side, onto the sheets, all piled in a wild
topography at the side of the bed, and I
was still inside of you, while your wild cloud of dark
hair apostrophized the ball on the near post. It burns,
it cools, it rests, it rages; I shout in canyons, echoes
loud enough for any mountain top. A pillow whisperer.
I made love to you again. Now you are so far
away, oh my love. Playing at death, that endless,
careening fall; and yet I am still inside of you.

2025

Auto Wreck

His boots stood still in the floorboard, but he
was gone already, airborne and flying to the grave;
a tumble into the past. It's the way the world
is lost. The universe contracted to a point
somewhere in the region of the navel. His car
bounced, then bounced once more, slid awhile,

then rolled several times. The tires blew out
somewhere in all that, but by then, he was dead.
Six quarts of watery cottage cheese, confining
the upper and nether limits of whomsoever
it was, locked within a metaphorical space, perhaps
metaphysical, too, flowing down the pavement.

I say all this is a tale of many days, not only this singular
moment of violence. He's gone. Poor fool. That's it.

2025

Cold Fire

I am as much of flesh as any other thing. But will I ever
be part of a woman's soul? No, I think. I will never
be still. I loved her body. I loved her body too well.

That it not be lost in time, like tears in rain. They say
things like that in movies. A woman says it's sweet how
much she loved him. Or was it the easy way he pleasured

her? The strength of his body doing it? On the
other hand, she was a morning person, fond of that hour
for love. Women don't know what a chore it is, even
as it makes us cry out with the joy in it. But love? That's
no charm. What ever burned but left no trace? Be still.
I'll hear your great heart beating. Like solemn children, we

await the ice cream truck. Love sits heavy the
chest, and pays for all our breath with only two coins.

2025

Wedded Bliss

You don't want to wait for Sis, you know, who
awaits us outside with the children and the
husband of the bride, whose blissful ignorance
bespeaks a carnal knowledge of assorted
bridesmaids. All parties must occupy the proper
social space in this universe, lest Yahweh become
incensed.
        That one is one bridesmaid in question
—the one in the ugly dress, done for now with
dying her littlest death possible, not once
but several times, with the groom. So near the
cost of what is elsewhere bartered. Her cries could
be heard in the vestibule, up the middle
of the nave, throughout the congregation, into
the sanctuary. Thus the course of true love.

2025

A Busy Monster

The book of love poems I've read in one by one
for so long, and wished I had written every one
to read to you, or so I said, is missing. Don't
lie, Sweet Thing. Since I didn't and don't have any
such feelings, I must be the deeper soul than any
of those that wrote what I've read. You took it. No other
words could've said it better, could they? Say it better
than has been already, and not once but many times,
with no sense of what is best, and he's not in just
now, come back later. The prickling, electric smoothness
of your flesh next to mine. Pity him not, this busy
monster. Dudley and the Queen, caught in the tortured
bloodways of an infarcted heart. The sweet effulgence
of her liquid slot. I guess that it will have to do.

2025

Maggie

Maggie had a smoke in the stairwell, beyond
the open doors at the back. I joined her there; she gazed
on me with yearning, as I her, victims of our own hungers.

Hungers like that run in packs, like wolves or dogs.
Teeth and an appetite with swift feet and red-rimmed
eyes, intent on bringing down some doe-eyed thing.

Like Maggie. A brief enough battle over her, a battle
that marked no dubious success. My undefiled, my blandly
monochromatic sorrows. Passing to the left, says take

and eat. I wanted to ask, but was much too afraid. The
winter moistness outside beaded on the inside of
the glass. Another kind of window, refractory

of gray, that breaks apart like sodden paper. All I can
do is watch, and pray that the transplant takes.

2025

Militated

And she was a beauty. Could I still, if she
were not seized by this Pharaoh, search out the
borders of an endless, loveless desert
until she is found? Solomon knew, as long

ago as that. I don't need to send to ask.
Leave her vagrant at the threshold. One or
the other discarded heart, to be gnawed
by passing dogs. Run out like grief, salt

tears. All the gradients of grayscale
militate to the affirmative. Damn your
data, he said. Because I know that you are
there, and I'd have you know that I am here.

What grows in all this debonair disarray of
the violently dead, is entirely up to you.

2025

Stay With the Wind

A flat, *fortissimo* A, putting him in
not the mirrors but the echo chamber,
begging the question: where does the truth live?
Not on this planet, Bubba. Nor that one

over there, neither. Hanging fire is someone's
breast laid bare indeed, an open wound
inflicted upon dubious terms of
engagement; each moment flung on the blood

boiling hearth like gravy for a Sunday roast, and my
love is Scarlett standing over Tara.
Tomorrow, she says, is another day.
When will the whining bitch ever shut up?

Something archaic, maybe like a Dobro,
or an Armonica in an echo chamber.

2025

That Girl

So many girls considered you, thought of some
conditional parade the length of your thighs. That one,
that's last wanted to taste you. To want to press her
softness into your face. To allow you such access
would make you weep like a child. Wanted you to
grow hard in her hand, guide you inside of her, to sigh
in the back of her throat while you oh so gently nip
the crenellated quickening of her nipples. Wanted
your body to cleave unto hers, always on top.
To have you burst inside of her like some firework of
body and soul. No lame doggies there, nor cowgirls.
Wanted you to cry out into her mouth, her mouth
in yours. Wanted to kiss you, one long final act of
the day, and then to lie quietly watching you sleep.

2025

That Boy

So many boys lusted for you, dreamed of
some triumphant parade the length of your spine.
That one that's last wanted to taste you. Wanted
your softness to press his face into. To
suckle the round white gift of your breasts like
a child. Wanted to grow hard in your hands,
be guided inside of you, to bite oh
so gently the crenellated quickening
of your nipples. Wanted your body to
cleave unto his. To burst inside of you
like some firework of body and soul. Cry
out into your mouth, his mouth over yours. Wanted
to kiss you, one long final act of the day,
and to lie quietly beside you, and sleep.

2025

A Moderately Bad Date

They scurry like fleas in fur. They launch at escape
velocity, mere falling. Always rolling
down. Games you might win, prizes you might take,
but won't, and everywhere, the sure-footed tumble
of the gymnasts, shod with lead. In the wings;
a crab indeed. Down now, down they go, and
she down with them, angel in the mud. It seemed
as right as calling the cops on the fucking
idiot who hit you. I bet he fucked you
right after, too, didn't he? His idiot
way of apologizing. To you. You're
such a narcissistic cunt. You looked at
me just so. You'd re-enacted your own
rape, as if it were a moderately bad date.

2025

Slow Time

Bitterness at times is just too sweet,
its savor on the tongue too cloying sweet,
the notes struck back of the mouth, in the
sinuses too, too flavorful; better the

sharp bite of forgiveness, stinging
the tongue, the blood taste of slow time. And all
my yesterdays to light only one fool the way
to remember, not well but too, too wisely.

My discontents winter in Aruba,
along with the money. All history
discernible in traitors less grand than
Iago, but grander still than Judas. If so,
to the happy betterment of the local whores,
when he ought to have lived to be old.

2025

Biography

K. M. Clay—Kevin Mark—was born in Fort Worth, Texas, at St. Joseph's Hospital, in 1954, to Raymond, Sr. and Edna Clay. He was educated in the public schools of the Birdville District in Haltom City, graduating from Haltom High in 1972. He married in 1976 and had two sons, Mark and Patrick, with his first wife, Selma Sherry Trantham. Twenty years later, beginning in 1996, he attended Tarleton University in Stephenville, Texas, transferring in with 70-odd hours from the 1970s at Tarrant County College in Hurst, Texas, and the University of Texas at Arlington. By 1997, he had earned Bachelor's and a Master's degrees in English at Tarleton State University. In 1999, he graduated with a PhD in American Literature at the University of North Texas in Denton, Texas. He retired from teaching in 2021, and currently resides in Arlington, Texas with his wife, Elizabeth B. Clay. He recently published his first collection of poetry *Gravity Won: Selected Poems* (Romar Press).

www.ingramcontent.com/pod-product-compliance
Lightning Source LLC
Chambersburg PA
CBHW061126100726

47911CB00013B/694